Battle on Two Fronts
1944-45

Text by Tom Cockle
Color plates by Douglas Jameson

Copyright © 2007
by CONCORD PUBLICATIONS CO.
10/F, B1, Kong Nam Industrial Building
603-609 Castle Peak Road
Tsuen Wan, New Territories
Hong Kong
www.concord-publications.com

We welcome authors who can help
expand our range of books. If you
would like to submit material,
please feel free to contact us.

We are always on the look-out for new,
unpublished photos for this series.
If you have photos or slides or
information you feel may be useful to
future volumes, please send them to us
for possible future publication.
Full photo credits will be given upon
publication.

ISBN 962-361-077-7
printed in Hong Kong

Introduction

By the beginning of 1944, the once victorious German Army was being pushed back on all fronts. The German 6.Armee had surrendered at Stalingrad in February 1943. The losses were staggering. It is estimated that 300,000 Germans, 200,000 Rumanians, 130,000 Italians and 120,000 Hungarians were either killed or captured. In May of 1943, the Germans had surrendered in North Africa and another 250,000 men were taken into captivity. The attempt to turn the tide on the Eastern Front at Kursk in July 1943 had ended disastrously. British, Canadian and American Armies had landed in Sicily in July 1943 and after capturing the island, had jumped over to the mainland and had already advanced as far as Cassino by the end of the year. The initiative had permanently passed over to the Allied Armies.

Following their success at Kursk, the Soviet Army continued to strike at the German front. They re-captured the city of Kharkov in August and by the end of October had established a bridgehead over the Dnepr River and cut off the German forces still holding the Crimean Peninsula. In the north, they had pushed the Germans back into the Baltic States and Byelorussia.

In March 1944, a massive attack in the south had pushed the German Armies almost back to the pre-war borders of Poland and Romania. The spring rains and general exhaustion brought a halt to operations and both sides prepared for the inevitable Russian summer offensive.

In the meantime, in northern France, the Germans continued defensive preparations for the Allied invasion, expected to take place at Calais.

The Battle of Normandy started a few minutes after midnight on 6 June 1944, when British, Canadian and American airborne forces landed in France. Initially, the Germans were slow to react, still under the impression that Calais was to be the site of the main thrust. Within a few days, however, Panzer units stationed in France and Belgium were ordered into battle but too late to stem the tide of Allied troops and material pouring into the bridgehead.

The German Army fiercely contested every inch of ground gained in the first weeks of battle but was unable to stop the surging Allied forces. In early July, the American forces were finally able to break through the weakened German defenses in the west and began to move east, trapping the remaining Germans against the advancing British and Canadian forces between Falaise and Argentan. By 20 August 1944, the pocket was closed trapping some 50,000 German troops. The Battle of Normandy resulted in over 240,000 Germans killed or wounded and 200,000 missing or captured. Losses in equipment were also staggering: 1,500 armored vehicles, 3,500 artillery pieces and 20,000 other vehicles and while the Luftwaffe did not appear to contribute much to the defenses, 3,500 aircraft were also lost.

The German Armies retreated north and east across France, closely pursued by the victorious Allied forces.

Meanwhile, on the Eastern Front, the Soviet summer offensive, code named Operation 'Bagration', began on 10 June with attacks against Finland. On 23 June, attacks in Byelorussia resulted in the complete route of Army Group Center. This success was followed by the liberation of a substantial part of the Baltic region by the end of August. In the south, Army Group North Ukraine was defeated and Russian forces crossed the Vistula River, freeing most of the Ukraine and parts of Poland. They were now poised to strike at the borders of Germany itself. In three months, the German Army had lost some 917,000 men fighting on the Eastern Front. On 20 August, Soviet forces began a new offensive aimed at Army Group South Ukraine. In five days they surrounded the German forces which resulted in the loss of a further 500,000 men.

On 17 September, 1944, the Allies launched the largest airborne operation of the war when they parachuted into the Dutch cities of Arnhem, Eindhoven and Nijmegen under the code name Market-Garden, commanded by British Field Marshall Montgomery. The objective was to secure the major bridges over the rivers running through those cities that would allow ground forces to race north and secure them. If successful, this would provide a springboard from which an assault could be launched on the industrial centers of the Ruhr and hopefully bring the war to an end by Christmas. In the meantime, Patton's Third Army was halted some 60 miles from the German border in Eastern France, as critically needed supplies of gasoline were diverted to Montgomery's attack.

Unknown to Allied planners, elements of two SS-Panzer-Divisions were resting and refitting in the Arnhem area and although the British paratroops fought valiantly, they were soon overcome. The last bridge on the road to Germany had eluded the Allies grasp and Montgomery's forces were now faced with a long and arduous battle of attrition fought under poor weather conditions.

By the end of September, Soviet forces had liberated Rumania and reached the borders of Hungary and Yugoslavia. Further south, German forces were also driven out of Bulgaria. At the end of October, operations began against the Hungarian capital and on 26 December, 188,000 German troops were surrounded at Budapest. Several attempts were made to break through to the besieged troops but they were eventually destroyed in mid-February.

In September 1944 as the German Army was reeling back in disarray on all fronts, Adolf Hitler devised a plan that he felt could dramatically change the course of the war for Germany.

His plan, code named 'Wacht am Rhein', was to attack through the Ardennes towards Antwerp, against the weakest point of the American lines, during poor weather conditions, which would neutralize enemy air operations and provide the best opportunity for success. As six to eight weeks would be needed to raise and re-equip the necessary forces required for the undertaking, late November would be the earliest time the operation could begin.

The assault force would be made up of three armies with 8 Panzer and 15 Infantry Divisions. It was intended that these three armies would thrust through the American units holding the front, cross the Meuse River and continue on to Brussels and Antwerp.

German preparations went unnoticed by Allied intelligence so when the attack began with a massive hour-long artillery barrage, panic and confusion spread through the American units. When the bombardment ended, thousands of German soldiers advanced under the glow of searchlights bounced off the low clouds, bathing the battlefield in artificial moonlight.

It was expected 1.SS-Panzer-Korps would achieve the decisive breakthrough needed for success of the operation and for this, was given the greatest concentration of forces. Kampfgruppe Peiper made it as far as Stoumont before being halted by stubborn American resistance and fell back to La Gleize, where they were surrounded. On Christmas Eve, Peiper was granted permission to break out of the trap and early on Christmas morning, he and about 800 men escaped back to the German lines leaving all their equipment behind.

To the south, 2.Panzer-Division followed a route that took them around the north side of Bastogne and by the evening of 23 December, they were only four miles from the Meuse. Panzer-Lehr-Division attempted to reinforce that success but a British tank regiment was now in a blocking position at Dinant. The Americans succeeded in cutting off the two Kampfgruppen from the rest of the division. Low on fuel and ammunition, they were overwhelmed and eliminated on 26 December. This was to be the farthest advance achieved in the offensive.

In late December, the Germans mounted a final assault to try and capture Bastogne, but Patton's Third Army had already broken through to the beleaguered city.

On New Year's Day, the Germans launched a diversionary attack code named Operation 'Nordwind', in the Alsace region to attempt to divert American forces away from the Ardennes. At the same time, XIX.Armee attacked north towards Strasbourg in an attempt to break out from the Colmar Pocket, and link up with I.Armee, thereby trapping a substantial part of the U.S. VI and French II Corps. Allied resistance prevented the German forces from linking up and by the end of January, Operation 'Nordwind' was over.

'Wacht am Rhein' resulted in approximately 81,000 German and 77,000 Americans killed and wounded in addition to the loss of approximately 500-600 armored fighting vehicles on each side. By the end of January 1945 the Germans were back to where they had launched the attack six weeks earlier.

The Soviets launched their last, massive offensive simultaneously along five fronts running from the Baltic Sea to the Carpathian Mountains in January 1945. The Germans were quickly defeated in East Prussia and Pomerania. The Baltic ports of Danzig and Gdynia fell in March and the Soviets repulsed a major German attack near Lake Balaton in Hungary.

By February 1945, the western Allies were prepared to resume their drive into Germany. The offensive aimed to trap and destroy the retreating Germans on the west side of the Rhine before they had a chance to fall back across it. British and Canadian forces on the Allied left wing carried out the opening attack along the west bank of the Rhine. However, the delay caused by the Ardennes Offensive meant that the attack would now take place over ground that had begun to thaw. The Germans reacted by blowing up the dams on the Roer River causing massive flooding that delayed the Americans by two weeks. The Americans finally entered Cologne on 5 March but by then, the Germans had been able to evacuate most of their men and equipment back across the Rhine.

Further south, the U.S. First Army captured an intact railway bridge over the Rhine at Remagen, but the Allies could not exploit this success, as it would have meant a considerable adjustment in plans for the next stage in the campaign. Patton's Third Army broke through the German defenses in the Eifel and raced to Coblenz, where they wheeled south into the Palatinate trapping considerable German forces still facing the U.S. Seventh Army in Lorraine. On the night of 22 March, Patton's forces crossed the Rhine one day ahead of the scheduled assault by Montgomery's forces in the north.

Montgomery's assault went forward as planned on 23 March and the Rhine was crossed in four places. Two airborne divisions were dropped behind it the next day to consolidate the bridgeheads and soon, German resistance began to crumble and before long, collapsed completely.

The Allied armies swept eastward, crossing the Elbe River on 29 April and on 2 May, were on the Baltic coast.

In early March, the Russians were held on the east bank of the Oder River although they had forced a small bridgehead at Küstrin. Further south, Russian forces continued their advance and entered Vienna in early April. On 16 April, the Soviets broke out of their bridgehead and by 25 April, had completely surrounded Berlin. Although Hitler had committed suicide on 30 April, fighting still raged on until the final surrender a week later.

The war in Europe ended officially at midnight on 8 May 194.

Western Front - Normandy to Berlin

Two photos of an Sd.Kfz.10/5 from an unknown unit parked on a Norman roadside in the early days of the invasion. This is the unarmored version mounting the 2cm Flak 38, although the identifying feature was not the gun, but the width of the gun platform and on this example, the fender can be seen to flare out over the drive sprocket. Initially, they were issued to independent anti-aircraft battalions in the both the Heer and Luftwaffe but in 1942, they were authorized as part of a Panzer-Regiment or Abteilung. In the second photo, a rarely photographed 2cm Flak 38 auf Selbsfahrlafette Zgkw.3t (Sd.Kfz.11) is coming into view. The gun is missing but the shape of the armored front, similar to the Sd.Kfz.251, is unmistakable.

An Sd.Kfz.7/1, mounting the formidable 2cm Flakvierling 38, from an unknown SS unit sits manned and ready for action. This particular vehicle is fitted with the armored cab, part of which can be seen on the lower right of the photo. In practice, the gun could fire up to 800 rounds per minute, which increased the chances of hitting high-speed fighter aircraft. Almost 900 units were completed from April 1940 to December 1944.

The Flakpanzer IV 'Möbelwagen' was armed with the 3.7cm Flak 43 mounted on a Pz.Kpfw.IV Ausf.J chassis. The first twenty units were completed in March 1944 and the following June, eight were issued to each of the 9., 11. and 116.Panzer-Divisions in the west. A total of 240 units were produced by March 1945.

Another new anti-aircraft weapon in the Wehrmacht arsenal, was the 'Wirbelwind' mounting the 2cm Flakvierling 38. The first 17 were completed in July 1944 and, starting in September, began to be issued to the Pz.-Fla Zug of the Panzer units on the basis of four 'Wirbelwind' and four 'Möbelwagen' each.

The body of a German soldier lays out on the engine deck of an Sd.Kfz.251/9 Ausf.C somewhere in Normandy. The vehicle is unusual as it is fitted with an additional armored plate running down the top of the crew compartment as extra protection from small arms fire. The vehicle mounted the 7.5cm KwK37, which was made obsolete in the Pz.Kpfw.IV by the introduction of the Kwk40 L/43 gun, and were issued to the Panzer-Grenadier companies of the Panzer divisions.

A Pz.Kpfw.IV Ausf.J from 8./Pz.Rgt.3 of 2.Panzer-Division in Normandy in the days leading up to the invasion. The chassis number '89589' is stenciled on the front plate and indicates that this is one of the first Pz.Kpfw.IV Ausf.J manufactured in February 1944 by Nibelungwerk in Austria. This unit carried large white, stenciled outline tactical numbers on the sides and rear of the turret Schürzen and the divisional emblem, a white trident on the front and rear hull plates. On 10 June 1944, 2.Panzer-Division reported strength was 98 Pz.Kpfw.IV and 79 Panthers.

A Panther Ausf.A from I./Pz.Rgt.3 of 2.Panzer-Division burns south of Cheux on 27 June 1944 while another one lies abandoned in the background. The division lost seven Panthers in an assault on the town to relieve 8./SS-Pz.Rgt.12.

Two Panther Ausf.G from II./Pz.Rgt.33 of 9.Panzer-Division are loaded on rail transport for the journey to Normandy from its base in southern France after the invasion. On 10 June 1944, the divisions reported strength was 78 Pz.Kpfw.IV and 40 Panthers.

A Panzerbefehlswage V Panther Ausf.A fror II./Pz.Rgt.33 o 9.Panzer-Division i Normandy. The divisio suffered heavy losse on its journey to th invasion front an served for only abou two weeks at th beginning of Augus Judging from the battl scarred condition of thi vehicle, it was involve in some intens fighting. This is an earl production Ausf.A a indicated by th horizontal jack mount.

A Panther Ausf.G, probably from II./Pz.Rgt.33 of 9.Panzer-Division, parked on a street somewhere in eastern France in the fall of 1944. The three-digit tactica number '635' can be seen painted in red with a white outline on the side of the turret. This unit was the only one in France until very late in 1944, that organized their Panthers into the II.Abteilung.

Two photos of a Pz.Kpfw.IV Ausf. H from I./Pz.Rgt.22 of 21.Panzer-Division captured along the road from Caen to Lebisey on 3 July 1944. The division fielded a total of 112 Pz.Kpfw.IV at the beginning of the Normandy campaign including 22 earlier short barrel versions. This early production vehicle is unusual in that it has an additional 30mm armor plate bolted to the lower hull while the front plate on the upper hull is the one-piece 80mm plate introduced in June 1943 and does not have the Zimmerit coating.

A Borgward BIV Ausf.A (Sd.Kfz.301) remote control demolition vehicle from Panzer Kompanie 315 (Fkl) captured near Bénouville north of Caen. On 15 January 1944, the unit was attached to 21.Panzer-Division and at the end of April 1944, was stationed near Sassy, 35 kilometers southeast of Caen. On the rear plate, the chalked marking of the British 51st (Highland) Infantry Division, a circle around the letters 'HD' can be seen along with the tactical sign for Pz.Kp.315 (Fkl), a white stenciled rhomboid with a circle beside it.

A Pz.Kpfw.IV Ausf.H from II./Pz.Lehr.Rgt.130 of Panzer-Lehr-Division, sits on the roadside south of Bayeux. An M4 DD (Duplex Drive), or Sherman II as it was known in the British Army, is seen heading toward the front lines beside it. Records indicate that 8th Armoured Brigade was the only British unit equipped with the Sherman II DD in Normandy.

Two photos of a Panther Ausf.A from I./Pz.Rgt.6 of Panzer-Lehr-Division knocked out by the British 50th Division along the road northwest of Tilley-sur-Seulle near Bernières on 12 June 1944. At the beginning of the invasion, Panzer-Lehr-Division fielded 88 Panthers.

On 14 June 1944, this Panther Ausf.A was one of six Panthers lost to I./Pz.Rgt.6 of Panzer-Lehr-Division at Lingèvres, 3.5 kilometers west of Tilley-sur-Seulles. Barely recognizable under the soot blackened side of the turret is the tactical number '225', painted in red with a white outline.

This Panther Ausf.A from I./Pz.Rgt.6 of Panzer-Lehr-Division, was knocked out near Hottot-les-Bagues, southwest of Tilley-sur-Seulles on the night of 15/16 June 1944 during an attack to retake the village. The regimental commander's Panther was also lost that night.

An armored column with Panthers and SPW waits along a French country lane while a commander's conference is held to plan the next attack. This is an early Panther Ausf.A with the 'letter box' machine gun port on the glacis, which was later replaced by a ball mount. It was common for the Panther crews from I./Pz.Rgt.6 of Panzer-Lehr-Division to paint the name of a girl on the bottom of the gun travel lock and here we see the name 'Christel'.

A Panther Ausf.A and a Schwere Panzerpähwagen (5cm) (Sd.Kfz.234/2) 'Puma' armored reconnaissance vehicle from Panzer-Lehr-Division sit abandoned in the vicinity of Canisey, near St. Lô around 25/26 July 1944. Just barely visible on the side of the Panther turret is the tactical number '300', which was painted in red with a white outline, indicating that this was the company commander's vehicle. The 'Puma' would have belonged to Pz.Aufkl.Lehr-Abt.130.

Panther Ausf.A from I./SS-Pz.Rgt.1 from 1.SS-Panzer-Division 'LSSAH' seen in a Belgian town during the spring of 1944, where it was resting and refitting after the devastating losses on the Russian Front the year before. At this time their reported strength was 98 Pz.Kpfw.IV and 79 Panthers.

One of the first five production Tiger II Ausf.B issued to Pz.Kp.316 (Fkl) and assigned to 1./s.Pz.Kp. (Fkl) from Panzer-Lehr-Division, lies abandoned near Chateaudun. The Tigers suffered from many mechanical breakdowns and most were abandoned by their crews, having seen limited action against the advancing U.S. Army in mid-August 1944.

The division was entrained for the Normandy area in mid-June 1944, where they were assembled south of Caen. While some of the units were immediately committed to battle, the greater part of the division was not in the line until after 9 July 1944. In this photo, Panthers of 1.Abteilung have been loaded on the trains that will take them to Normandy from their rest area near Beverlo in Belgium and have been interspersed with the divisional transport to minimize the risk from an aerial attack.

A Pz.Kpfw.IV Ausf.J from II./SS-Pz.Rgt.2 from 2.SS-Panzer-Division 'Das Reich', lies burned out in a field near St. Lô in late June or early July 1944. In April 1944, the division was stationed in southern France near Toulouse and was ordered to Normandy shortly after the Allied landings. Their progress was delayed by constant attacks from the Maquis and several hundred civilians were executed in reprisal.

A late model StuG.III Ausf.G of II./SS-Pz.Rgt.10 from 10.SS-Panzer-Division 'Frundsberg' sits camouflaged under a canopy of tall trees over a French road as protection against Allied fighter-bombers. At this time, the Panzer regiment consisted of two companies equipped with Pz.Kpfw.IV and two with Sturmgeschütz III. The waffle pattern Zimmerit coating indicates that this vehicle was assembled at the Alkett plant in Berlin.

Three photos of 'Wespe' self-propelled light field howitzers of SS-Pz.Art.Rgt.10 from 10.SS-Panzer-Division 'Frundsberg' while they were stationed in France during the winter of 1943-44. Built on the modified chassis of the Pz.Kpfw.II, the 'Wespe' mounted the 10.5cm leFH18/2 and were issued to the Panzer-Artillerie-Regiments of the Panzer and Panzer-Grenadier Divisions.

The crews from 5.Kompanie of II./SS-Pz.Rgt.12 from 12.SS-Panzer-Division 'Hitlerjugend', line up in front of their new Pz.Kpfw.IV Ausf.H for inspection. The vehicles are painted in Dunkelgelb RAL 7028 with a camouflage scheme of Rotbraun RAL 8017 and Olivgrün RAL 6003 patches sprayed randomly over the Zimmerit anti-magnetic mine paste. At this time, the three digit tactical numbers were painted in a black-stenciled outline. The crewmen are wearing the black leather U-Boat jacket and trousers, which had been originally provided to the Italian Navy and were brought back to Germany by 1.SS-Panzer-Division 'Leibstandarte' in the fall of 1943.

A new Pz.Bef.Wg.IV Ausf.H parked alongside a road on the way to the invasion front. A 2m 'Sternantenne D' (star antenna) for the Fu 8 radio set can be seen mounted where the normal antenna was mounted which, along with the lack of a tactical number on the turret skirt, would indicate this is probably a II.Bataillon command vehicle. Production of the Pz.Bef.Wg.IV. started in March 1944 with 88 units being converted from rebuilt Panzer IV's. Records indicate that the division was issued with 5 on 30 April 1944. The divisional emblem of the 12.SS-Panzer-Division can be seen painted in white on the right mudguard.

Two Pz.Kpfw.IV Ausf.H roll across an open field followed by an Sd.Kfz.251 Ausf.C. The vehicle on the right is also a Pz.Bef.Wg.IV but with the star antenna, barely visible on the original photograph, mounted to a special armored housing welded on the upper right rear of the hull. Another Pz.Kpfw.IV can be seen parked in the background.

A Universal Carrier being used as an ambulance by the Durham Light Infantry, passes a knocked out Panther Ausf.A from 2.Kompanie, 12.SS-Panzer-Division 'Hitlerjugend' north of Rauray in late June 1944. Assuming each company in I.Bataillon used the same tactical numbering sequence, then '204' would have belonged to the company commander, SS-Obersturmführer Gaede.

Another view of Panther '204' with a column of Sherman tanks passing by heading in the direction of Évrecy from Tilley-sur-Seulles. Note the tactical number painted on the 'C' tow hook carried on the side of the hull.

A Panther Ausf.A from 1./SS Pz.Rgt.12 lies upside dow beside the road betwee Norrey-en-Bessin an Bretteville-l'Orgueilleuse where it was overturned b Allied engineers to clear th road. An anti-tank gu knocked it out on 8 Jun 1944 but most of the damag was caused when explosiv trials were conducted on th hulk at a later date.

Canadian troops examine the wreckage of a Panther Ausf.G from 4./SS-Pz.Rgt.12 destroyed by a PIAT bomb in Bretteville-l'Orgueilleuse during a night attack on 8 June 1944. The damage to the rear of the turret was caused when another Panther following fired into it in the confusion of battle. This photo was taken around 20 June 1944.

A Panther Ausf.G from 1./SS-Pz.Rgt.12, smolders at Fontenay-le-Pesnil late June 1944. In the foreground, is a burned out M4 composite h Sherman that was probably knocked out by the Panther before it wa destroyed itself. On 26 June, Sherman tanks from the Sherwood Range Yeomanry advanced past Fontenay-le-Pesnil and were in Cheux by noon.

Three Panthers from 1./SS-Pz.Rgt.12 maneuver their w around a farmhouse at Fontenay-le-Pesnil in early June 194 On 11 June 1944, 2.Kompanie counter-attacked to t northwest of the village destroying seven tanks from Squadron of the 4/7 Dragoon Guards.

A Pz.Kpfw.IV Ausf.H from 8./SS-Pz.Rgt.12 is towed away by a Centaur ARV from the British 11th Armoured Division after being captured near Cheux. The divisional emblem, a raging bull, can be seen on the front plate. This Panzer IV, with the tactical number '837', was commanded by SS-Untersturmführer Jeran and took part in the successful action at le Menil-Patry on 11 June where 37 Sherman tanks from the 6th Armoured Regiment (First Hussars) were knocked out.

A Panther Ausf.G from 1./SS-Pz.Rgt.12 makes its way through the demolished city of Caen in July 1944. On the evening of 7 July, 500 Allied bombers took part in a devastating air raid over Caen to soften up the German defenses for the beginning of Operation 'Charnwood', which was meant to drive the Germans out and finally capture the city. On the night of 8 July, the division began to pull out of Caen to form a new defensive line on the south bank of the Orne.

The division conducted a fighting withdrawal through Belgium and was sent back to Germany to rest and refit in late September 1944. This new Sd.Kfz.251/7 Ausf.D from 12.SS-Panzer-Division 'Hitlerjugend' is pictured in the fall of 1944. The vehicle is painted in Dunkelgelb RAL 7028 with a camouflage scheme of Rotbraun RAL 8017 and Olivgrün RAL 6003 patches and has the division's emblem painted in white beside the right vision flap.

A heavily camouflaged StuG.IV of SS-Pz.Abt.17 from 17.SS-Panzer-Grenadier-Division 'Götz von Berlichingen' rolls along a country road near Carentan during the first week of the invasion. The Abteilung was equipped with three companies of Sturmgeschütz and was the only unit in Normandy equipped with the StuG.IV. Most StuG.IV production was allocated as single companies to the infantry divisions.

Two photos of Tiger '213' from 2./s.Pz.Abt.503 as it rolls through Bourgthéroulde towards the Seine River after escaping destruction in the Falaise Pocket, 12 August 1944. The battalion was in training at Ohrdruf when it was ordered to Normandy, arriving east of Caen on 6 July 1944 with two companies equipped with Tiger Is and one company of the new Tiger II. Most of the vehicles that made it to Rouen during the retreat would be unable to cross the river and were abandoned.

Sd.Kfz.7 half-track prime mover also makes its way through Bourgthéroulde towards the Seine towing, what looks to be a heavily camouflaged 15cm sIG33 gun.

An Sd.Kfz.251/8 Ausf.D, the ambulance version of this armored half-track, clatters past the church Bourgthéroulde, carrying German wounded towards safety. In addition to the prominent Red Cross markings on the side of the hull, a large red cross flag has been draped across the open top of the vehicle to identify it to Allied fighter–bombers.

Another Sd.Kfz.251/8 Ausf.D, captured intact by British forces is cleaned up and has received a fresh coat of olive drab paint, leaving the Red Cross markings intact. It was a common practice for both sides to impress captured vehicles in good working order into service.

Two photos of new Tiger IIs from 3./s.Pz.Abt.503 conducting firing trials at Mailley-le-Camp, east of Paris. The company had been withdrawn in late July a sent there to be re-equipped. On 11 August 1944, the company was entrained for the journey back to Normandy, however, their train was attacked by All fighter-bombers with the loss of several men and one Tiger. By this time the German Army was in full retreat and the unit never made it back to Normand

In May 1944, the Tigers of s.SS-Pz.Abt.101 held live firing exercis near Amiens in France. Pictured here facing the camera are S Untersturmführer Iriohn, SS-Sturmbannführer Von Westernhagen a SS-Obersturmführer Raasch.

A crewman from s.Pz.Abt.503 points out the punishment absorbed by the 100mm thick, sloped armor plates of the Tiger II that resulted only in deep gouges and chipped Zimmerit coating, but did not otherwise cause any damage.

Tiger '133' from 1./s.SS-Pz.Abt.101, rolls through Morgny on the morning of 7 June 1944. The Tigers from this unit all displayed carefully applied, textbook camouflage paint schemes of Rotbraun RAL 8017 and Olivgrün RAL 6003 patches over the Dunkelgelb RAL 7028 base and neatly applied three digit tactical numbers.

Tiger '323' from 3./s.SS-Pz.Abt.101 makes its way to the front in Normandy on 7 June 1944, with SS-Hauptscharführer Barkhausen in the commander's cupola. The unit had an operational strength of 37 Tigers at this time.

Tiger '222' is seen here towing disabled Tiger '231' away from Villers-Bocage on 14 June 1944, the day after SS-Obersturmführer Michael Wittmann spectacular victory against a tank battalion from the 4th County of London Yeomanry. The towing Tiger has often been misidentified as '211' or '232' but in th original photo, the last digit can be seen to be a '2', thereby eliminating the possibility of it being '211' and in another photo of '232', the unit insignia can b clearly seen to be painted on a patch of the bare hull from which the Zimmerit has been removed and this Tiger has it painted onto the Zimmerit.

is Tiger I from 1./s.SS-Pz.Abt.101 has been recovered by British soldiers in running condition. The unit insignia can be seen on the left side of the front ate but the 1.Kompanie insignia, a white rhomboid with a script 'S' inside and a '1' beside it, which was painted on the right side of the front plate, has been bliterated during its short time in combat. Note how shell splinters have damaged the Zimmerit coating, leaving the ochre colored Zimmerit highlighted ainst the undamaged painted areas. In the background can be seen the Panther Ausf.A from 2.Kompanie, 12.SS-Panzer-Division 'Hitlerjugend' with the rret number '204' seen previously.

ger '334' from 3./s.SS-Pz.Abt.101 was abandoned on e road from Rauray to Tilley-sur-Seulles. This Tiger as commanded by SS-Oberscharführer Rolf von esternhagen, who was the battalion commander's other. It was later recovered by the British, apparently good running order.

A column of Tigers from 2./s.SS-Pz.Abt.102 on its way to the Normandy area, liberally covered with cut foliage to camouflage its shape from Allied fight bombers. At the beginning of the Normandy campaign, s.SS-Pz.Abt.102 was stationed in Holland and was ordered to an area south of Calais on 13 Jun When it was finally realized by the German High Command that Calais was not the primary invasion site, the unit was ordered to make its way to Norman on 1 July 1944. At the time, they only had 28 Tigers available of their normal allotment of 45.

A battery of 15c Panzerwerfer 42 auf (Sd.Kfz.4/1) led by a Sd.Kfz.250/3 (Ne passes through French village on way to the front in Ju 1944. The Panzerwerf 42 was fitted with a te barrel rocket launche the 15cm Nebelwerf 42. Due to th conspicuous smok trails left by th projectiles it wa necessary to move th weapon immediate after firing to avo enemy counter fire.

The 15cm Nebelwerfer 42 projectiles weighed 34 kilograms and had a range of 6,900 meters. The rockets were not very accurate and the Germans relied on blanketing the area with a heavy concentration of fire. Armored vehicles were practically immune to all but a direct hit but unprotected infantry were more susceptible to the explosive force of the blast, the thin casings providing little in the way of fragmentation.

As the Allies approached Paris in mid-August of 1944, members of the Resistance and Communist party called for an uprising against the Germans left in the city. Here, a burned out Panther Ausf.A, possibly from either I./Pz.Rgt.6 from Panzer-Lehr-Division or I./Pz.Rgt.24 of 116.Panzer-Division, is surrounded by jubilant civilians in the Place de la Concorde after the surrender of the city. The Panther was disabled when it was rammed by a Sherman tank of the French 2ème Division Blindée after its HE shell failed to knock it out.

A Panther Ausf.G and a Panther Ausf.A from I./Pz.Rgt.24 of 116.Panzer-Division. The division had fought the Normandy battles without its Panther Abteilung, which had been transferred to Pz.Bde.111 in the spring. The division had been given I./Pz.Rgt.24 as its replacement Panther-Abteilung but they did not join up with them until August.

A battle scarred Panther Ausf.G from I./Pz.Rgt.24 of 116.Panzer-Division sits abandoned beside a French café during the late summer of 1944. The Panthers from this unit are noted for carrying spare road wheels bolted to the back of the turret and relocating the gun cleaning rod tube onto the back of the engine deck. Another unique trait is the Jerrycan racks attached to the rear of the hull inside of the rear stowage bins.

On 17 September 1944, the Allies launched the largest airborne assault of the war against three objectives in Holland – Arnhem, Nijmegen and Eindhoven. Allied intelligence had failed to detect that the 9.SS-Panzer-Division 'Hohenstaufen' and 10.SS-Panzer-Division 'Frundsberg' were resting and refitting in the Arnhem drop zone. Here we see a column of SS troops mounted in Sd.Kfz.250 (Neu) half-tracks accompanied by two officers with a captured airborne Jeep.

A column of Panthers from I./Pz.Rgt. 24 of Panzer-Brigade 111 approaches the town of Jures in eastern France on 20 September 1944. Following the breakout from Normandy, Lt.Gen. George S. Patton's Third Army swept towards the western border between France and Germany. In early September, Patton's forces were halted when the Allied High Command diverted gasoline supplies to support the main thrust north with Montgomery's 21st Army Group. The Germans assembled a large armored force including I./Pz.Rgt. 24, formerly of 16.Panzer-Division, now assigned to Panzer-Brigade 111, to strike at the flank of the American forces.

Panthers from I./Pz.Rgt. 24 of Panzer-Brigade 111 on the streets of Jures on 20 September 1944. On the day before, Panzer-Brigade 111, supporting Panzer-Brigade 113, was to have attacked Arracourt but lost their way during the night and played no part in the day's battle.

Grenadiers climb aboard a Panther Ausf.G from I./Pz.Rgt. 24 of Panzer-Brigade 111. The device being held by one of them is a mine detector and the operator with the battery pack on his back can be seen climbing up on the right. At the end of the battle, Panzer-Brigade 111 was left with seven tanks and 80 men out of 90 tanks and 2,500 men that they started with.

The remains of a Panther Ausf.G from an unknown unit, knocked out near Nancy in November 1944 by the 603rd Tank Destroyer Battalion from the 6th Armored Division.

This StuG.III Ausf.F/8 is from 11.Panzer-Division and was photographed in Beaume-les-Dames on 12 September 1944. Another photo of this vehicle shows that the division's ghost emblem was painted on the left side of the lower hull plate and another national cross was on the front plate to the right of the gun. The tactical number '001' is likely painted in black with a white outline.

Panzer IV Ausf.J from an unknown Panzer-Division is examined by curious U.S. troops in Southern France in the late summer of 1944. The first two digits the tactical number '71' can be faintly seen behind the national cross on the turret skirt armor.

ter being almost totally destroyed in France during the summer of 1944, s.Pz.Abt.503 was re-equipped with 43 new Tiger II tanks at Paderborn in September 44. The battalion was assembled for propaganda photographs before being transported to Hungary on 12 October 1944. Here, the commander of Kompanie in Tiger '300' parades in front of the rest of the battalion. His tank is painted in a classic three-color camouflage scheme while some others have e 'ambush' scheme.

A heavily camouflaged StuG.IV near Aachen in the fall of 1944. The soldier in the foreground is wearing the Army splinter pattern camouflage smock while other wear a variety of uniforms. The NCO on the left is armed with the relatively new MP44.

StuG.III Ausf.Gs from either StuG.Bde.341 or 394 in Würselen, north of Aachen, in October 1944. Both units fought in the area after Aachen had been surrounded by Allied troops in September and some of the hardest fighting took place around Würselen and the Hürtgen Forest. After suffering severe losses in France, both units were re-equipped with new Sturmgeschütz. These ones were manufactured by the Alkett Plant in Berlin, which was the only manufacturer producing vehicles with waffle pattern Zimmerit.

Flakpanzer 38(t) Ausf.L, SS-Flak-Abteilung 12, 12.SS-Panzer-Division 'Hitlerjugend', Normandy, June 1944
February 1944, twelve Flakpanzer 38(t) were issued to this unit and were still painted in their factory coat of Dunkelgelb RAL 7028. The only ∟ible markings were the standard Balkenkreuz painted on the sides of the superstructure.

K 45.01 (P), Stabs-Kompanie, s.H.Pz.Jg.Abt.653, Galicia, July 1944
⌐s is the only Panzerkampfwagen VI P to be used in combat. It is painted in Dunkelgelb RAL 7028 with a camouflage scheme of Rotbraun RAL 17 and Olivgrün RAL 6003 patches. The three digit tactical number is painted in red with a white outline on the sides of the turret and also ⌐ppeared on the top right of the rear plate. The unit insignia was also painted on the front and rear hull plate.

Panzerkampfwagen 'Maus', Böblingen, Germany, July 1944
An incomplete Maus turret was mounted on a chassis in June 1944, in preparation for an inspection by Generaloberst Guderian. The vehicle wo
painted in Dunkelgelb RAL 7028 with camouflage scheme of Rotbraun RAL 8017 and Olivgrün RAL 6003 wavy lines.

Tiger II, 3./s.SS.Pz.Abt.501, Ardennes, December 1944
This Tiger II was painted in Dunkelgelb RAL 7028 with a camouflage scheme of Rotbraun RAL 8017 and Olivgrün RAL 6003 patches. The larg
three-digit tactical numbers for 3.Kompanie were light blue with a yellow outline.

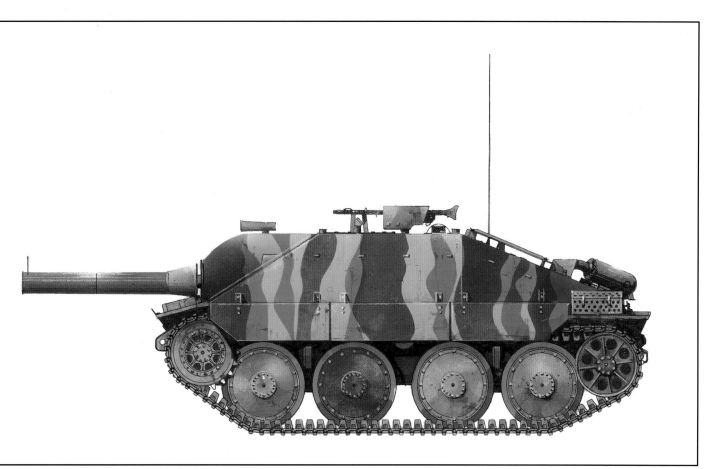

Flammpanzer 38(t), Panzer-Flamm-Kompanie 352, Ardennes, December 1944
Twenty Jagdpanzer 38(t) were converted to Flammpanzer for the Ardennes Offensive and issued to Panzer-Flamm-Kompanie 352 and 353. They were painted in Dunkelgelb RAL 7028 with a wavy, hard-edged camouflage scheme of Rotbraun RAL 8017 and Olivgrün RAL 6003 stripes.

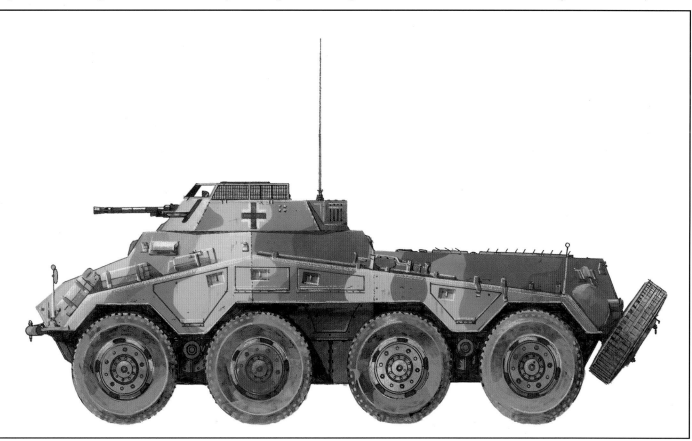

Schwerer Panzerpähwagen (2cm) (Sd.Kfz.234/1), Pz.Aufkl.Abt.4, 4.Panzer-Division, Danzig, Poland, January 1945
This vehicle is painted in Dunkelgelb RAL 7028 and has a hard-edged camouflage scheme of Rotbraun RAL 8017 and Olivgrün RAL 6003 patches. There are no markings other than the vehicle license number, WH-1868316, painted on the front and rear plate and a small Balkenkreuz painted on the side of the turret.

Jagdtiger, 3./s.H.Pz.Jg.Abt.653, Morsbronn, Germany, March 1945
This Jagdtiger is one of only twelve constructed using the Porsche suspension. It is painted in Dunkelgelb RAL 7028 with a camouflage schem
of Rotbraun RAL 8017 and Olivgrün RAL 6003 patches. The three-digit tactical number, '314', is painted in black.

Jagdtiger, 1./s.H.Pz.Jg.Abt.653, Schwetzingen, Germany, March 1945
This Jagdtiger is painted in Dunkelgelb RAL 7028 with a camouflage scheme of Rotbraun RAL 8017 and Olivgrün RAL 6003 patches. The three-
digit tactical number, '115', is painted in black.

Jagdpanther, 2./s.H.Pz.Jg.Abt.654, Ruhr Pocket, Germany, March 1945
Several Jagdpanther from this unit were destroyed by their crews after running out of fuel in the Ruhr Pocket in March 1945. This one is painted in Dunkelgelb RAL 7028 with a camouflage scheme of Rotbraun RAL 8017 and Olivgrün RAL 6003 patches. The three-digit tactical number is painted black with a white outline.

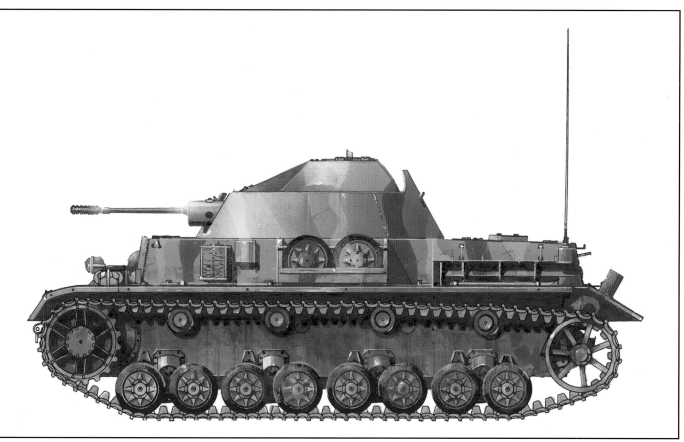

Flakpanzer IV 'Kugelblitz', unknown unit, Berlin, April 1945
Only two Flakpanzer IV 'Kugleblitz' were completed and rushed to Berlin in March 1945. It is speculated that the vehicle would have likely been painted in a base coat of Rot RAL 8012 primer with a hard-edged camouflage scheme of Dunkelgelb RAL 7028 and Olivgrün RAL 6003 patches.

Tiger I hybrid, Kompanie Fehrmann, Ostenholz, Germany, April 1945

Tiger-Kompanie Fehrmann was equipped with six Tiger I hybrids with early turrets and steel wheeled hulls. They were painted in Dunkelgelb RAL 7028 with camouflage scheme of Rotbraun RAL 8017 and Olivgrün RAL 6003 wavy lines. The tactical number 'F01' was crudely painted in white outline with an olive green center.

Sturmmörserwagen 606/4 mit 38cm Raketenwerfer 61, Sturm-Morser-Kompanie 1000, Elbe River area, spring 1945

This Sturmtiger is painted in Dunkelgelb RAL 7028 and has a camouflage scheme of Rotbraun RAL 8017 and Olivgrün RAL 6003 patches sprayed randomly over the base color and did not have Zimmerit coating.

Flakpanzer IV 'Möbelwagen' (Sd.Kfz.161/3), unknown FlaK.Art.Abt., Oder River area, spring 1945
This Möbelwagen was built on the chassis of a Pz.Kpfw.IV Ausf.J and is painted in Dunkelgelb RAL 7028 with a camouflage scheme of small Rotbraun RAL 8017 and large Olivgrün RAL 6003 patches. It is carrying the 3.7cm Flak43 anti-aircraft gun and is fitted with steel return rollers and the vertical 'Flammenvernichter' flame dampening exhaust.

Panther Ausf.G, unknown unit, Germany, spring 1945
This Panther Ausf.G is painted in the late war camouflage scheme of Olivgrün RAL 6003 with hard-edged patches of Dunkelgelb RAL 7028 and Rotbraun RAL 8017. It is fitted with the vertical 'Flammenvernichter' exhaust, raised cooling fan that provided heat to the crew compartment and the reinforced gun mantlet.

Pz.Kpfw.38(t), unknown unit, Poliãka, Bohemia, May 1945
It was very unusual to see an early vehicle of this type in use by the end of the war. This one is painted Dunkelgelb RAL 7028 with a camouflag
scheme of Rotbraun RAL 8017 and Olivgrün RAL 6003 spots. The only visible markings are a standard Balkenkreuz painted on the side of the turre

Schwerer Panzerpähwagen (7.5cm Pak 40) (Sd.Kfz.234/4), unknown unit, Germany 1945
This vehicle is painted in Dunkelgelb RAL 7028 and has a hard-edged camouflage scheme of Rotbraun RAL 8017 and Olivgrün RAL 6003 patche
Other than the standard Wehrmacht number plate on the front and rear, there are no other visible markings.

StuG.III Ausf.G and an Sd.Kfz.251/1 Ausf.D sit abandoned near Manhay, Belgium in late December 1944. This is a late production StuG.III without Zimmerit d equipped with the remote control machine gun mount on the fighting compartment roof, 80mm front plate on the right side of the superstructure, barrel vel support and deflector in front of the commander's cupola.

Sd.Kfz.250/1 (Neu) followed by an Sd.Kfz.234/3 from 116.Panzer-Division pass rough a German village near Aachen in the fall of 1944. The Sd.Kfz.234/3 mounted the 5cm Kwk51 L/24 and were issued to the reconnaissance companies of the Panzer visions to provide anti-tank support. A total of 88 were produced from June to ecember 1944.

A U.S. soldier poses for a picture with a Bergepanzer III knocked out in Belgium in the fall of 1944. In January 1944, all Panzer III returned for overhaul, were ordered converted to Bergepanzer and a total of 150 were completed from March to December 1944. Although this one has been converted from an Panzer III Ausf.J, it is fitted with the early style eight-hole drive sprocket with the spacer ring to accommodate the 40cm tracks.

Panzer-Grenadiers, wearing a variety [of] winter clothing, prepa[re] for an atta[ck] accompanied [by] Sd.Kfz.251/1 Ausf[.] half-tracks. To the l[eft] can be seen a la[te] production Sd.Kfz.251 Ausf.D equipped wi[th] the 7.5cm KwK37 L/[24] gun.

On 27 December 1.SS-Panzer-Division was relieved on the line by 18.Volks-Grenadier-Division and assembled between Vielsalm and Born, after which, they were transferred to V.Panzer-Armee. They had lost most of their armor with Kampfgruppe Peiper and what was left made their way south to join an attack against the Bastogne Corridor directed at Assenois. Here, two of the few remaining Panther Ausf.G available to 1.SS-Panzer-Division make their way south to join V.Panzer-Armee.

Two American soldie[rs] inspect a Panth[er] Ausf.G, possibly fro[m] 116.Panzer-Division, knocked out ne[ar] Houffalize, Belgium[,] January 1945. Th[is] division covered th[e] withdrawal of th[e] remnants of V.Panze[r-] Armee north of the tow[n] in mid-January an[d] barely escape[d] annihilation by the U.[S.] 2nd and 11th Armore[d] Divisions.

A U.S. Army officer poses in front of a knocked out Panther Ausf.G from Pz.Rgt.15 of 11.Panzer-Division in the Colmar area in late 1944. Another photo of this tank shows it had the tactical number '413' painted on the turret. Sherman tanks from the 43rd Tank Battalion of the 12th Armored Division destroyed the Panther. In the background, is a damaged Maginot Line fortification.

Two Bergepanther armored recovery vehicles abandoned somewhere on the Western Front. The one without the earth spade mounted on the rear is likely based on an Ausf.D chassis and does not appear to have Zimmerit while the one with the spade and Zimmerit is based on an early Ausf.A chassis. There were 240 Bergepanther produced on the Ausf.D and Ausf.A chassis from June 1943 to September 1944 with an additional 107 produced on Ausf.G chassis from September 1944 to March 1945.

A knocked out late StuG.III Ausf.G somewhere in Western Europe in the late fall of 1944 or early spring of 1945. The vehicle has taken a hit, low in the le[ft] side, which has blown off the first return roller and damaged the drive sprocket. It appears that part of the rear plate of the fighting compartment behind th[e] loader, has been neatly cut out for some unknown reason.

This is the famou[s] Panther Ausf.A fro[m] II./Pz.Rgt.33 9.Panzer-Division tha[t] was knocked out in fro[nt] of the Colog[ne] cathedral in Mar[ch] 1945. The Panther ha[d] knocked out tw[o] approaching Sherma[n] tanks when it wa[s] successfully taken [in] the flank by a T26E[4] Pershing tank from th[e] 32nd Armore[d] Regiment of the 3r[d] Armored Division. It [is] pictured here sometim[e] later after it had bee[n] towed around the sid[e] of the cathedral and le[ft] in front of the tra[in] station.

This Tiger I from Kompanie Hummel, has the distinction of having knocked out the first Pershing in Elsdorf, Germany on 25 February 1945. Kompanie Hummel was integrated into s.Pz.Abt.506 as its fourth company in December 1944. Other photos of the Tiger show it had the tactical number '201' painted in red or black with a white outline on the side of the turret. The Tiger was abandoned after becoming trapped in the debris of a ruined house as it tried to get away.

An MP poses beside a badly shot up Panther Ausf.G somewhere in Germany in early 1945. The raised fan tower on the engine deck indicates that this vehicle was fitted with the crew compartment heater introduced in October 1944.

Two U.S. servicemen pose with a Panther Ausf.A near Braunschweig, Germany in early 1945. The penetration hole from the shot that knocked it out can be seen just below the top of the engine deck. The resulting fire has burned away the Zimmerit coating on part of the hull and side of the turret.

Another derelict Panther Ausf.G photographed near Almen, Germany 1945. This Panther is fitted with the reinforced chin mantlet and appears be missing its gun barrel. Two faint numbers, '37', can be seen on the side the turret.

When the 11.Panzer-Division surrendered to U.S. forces in Bavaria on 4 May 1945, they turned over a number of late production Panther Ausf.G with late features like small welded loops on the turret for attaching foliage and lacking the anti-aircraft MG ring on the cupola. Pictured here are '411' and '421' along with a Panther Ausf.A in the background. Another photo of these two Panthers can be seen in the Concord book 'US Tank Battles' 7046 by Steve Zaloga.

his schwere Panzerpähwagen (2cm) Sd.Kfz.234/1 sits abandoned in a German town in 1945. These heavy armored cars were issued to the Panzer-
ufklärungs-Abteilung of the Panzer and Panzer-Grenadier divisions starting in July 1944. A total of 200 were produced from June 1944 to January 1945.

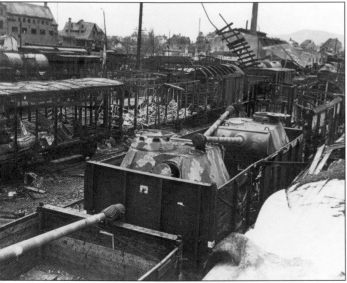

hese Panther turrets were photographed in the bombed out railway station
1 Aschaffenburg in 1945. The turret with the colorful camouflage paint
cheme is probably an Ausf.A production as it has the
ahverteidigungswaffe on the right rear of the turret roof but is lacking the
ilze socket. The other turret is obviously from an Ausf.D.

hree Jagdtigers from s.Pz.Jg.Abt.512 assembled in the town square in
serlohn, Germany on 16 April 1945 for a formal surrender ceremony to the
9th Infantry Division. Not visible in this photo are the two kill rings on the gun
arrel of the middle vehicle. The unit had been engaged in battle for several
ays around Paderborn with the U.S. 3rd Armored Division.

This early Tiger I was captured in Germany by the British Army and shipped to England for evaluation after the war. It has been fitted with the narrow transport tracks and is seen loaded on a Gotha 80 ton transporter with the wide battle tracks coiled up on the front of the trailer.

An Sd.Kfz.251/9 Ausf.D follows an Sd.Kfz.7/2 into captivity after the cessation of hostilities in 1945. The marking on the left rear of the Sd.kfz.251/9 looks like it may be the 'Windhund' emblem of 116.Panzer-Division. The gun barrel of the 3.7cm Flak 43 has been removed, probably to render the weapon inoperable

A column of American jeeps passes by an abandoned Sd.Kfz.11 half-track near the town of Berg Zabern on 23 March 1945. This vehicle has been fitted with an extended cab and a wooden cargo platform. Note the wire cutter welded to the front bumper of the Jeep.

Two photos of a Tiger II from s.Pz.Abt.506 taken near the town of Schmallenberg in the Sauerland in 1945. The first picture was probably taken early in the spring before the leaves were on the trees and second later in the summer after the tow cables and remaining tools had been stripped away.

An Sd.kfz.10/4 mounting the 2cm Flak 38 has stopped on a dirt road somewhere on the Eastern Front during the summer of 1944. The practical rate of fire was 180-220 rounds per minute and it had a maximum effective ceiling of 2200 meters.

The 2cm Flak 38 was also effective against ground targets such as machine guns at up to 2000 meters but the range was reduced to 300 meters against light armored vehicles.

A pair of Sd.Kfz.10/4, also mounting the 2cm Flak 38, fire at Russian aircraft flying over the German positions. A crew of seven manned the vehicle. There were 220 rounds of ammunition stowed in 20 round magazines in boxes mounted on the sides of the fold-down platform and on the gun itself. An additional 640 rounds was carried in a special two-wheel trailer, the Sd.Ah.51.

The Sd.Kfz.6/2 carried the 3.7cm Flak 36, which had a practical rate of fire of 80-100 rounds per minute. Although this was slower than the 2cm Flak, it had horizontal range of 6600 meters and a ceiling of 4800 meters. The Sd.Kfz.6/2 were issued almost exclusively to Luftwaffe Flak Regiments, the exception being 18 issued to Regiment 'Großdeutschland'.

The rider in a BMW R75 reconnaissance motorcycle combination gestures to the commander of an Sd.Kfz.251 Ausf.D half-track, probably to alert him to the presence of enemy forces ahead. The metal guards that normally protected the shock absorbers on the forks have been removed exposing the flexible bellows covering.

Heavily camouflaged Sd.Kfz.251/1 Ausf.D half-tracks from Panzer-Grenadier-Division 'Großdeutschland' pause by a lake in East Prussia in the fall of 1944. The third vehicle in the line appears to be an Sd.Kfz.251/17 Ausf.D although photographs exist of an Sd.kfz.251 Ausf.D mounting an MG 151/20 that was likely salvaged from a wrecked aircraft and this may be that vehicle as well.

Panzergrenadiers riding in an Sd.Kfz.251/1 Ausf.D roll past a knocked out Russian 76.2mm ZiS 3 Field Gun Model 1942 in the autumn of 1944. Many of these guns were captured by the Germans in 1942 and were re-chambered to take German ammunition and designated 7.62cm FK 288(r).

The crew of this Sd.Kfz.251/1 scramble aboard their vehicle during the winter of 1944-45. The half-track is finished in a coat of winter whitewash camouflage paint leaving a small rectangle of the base color where the tactical number '232' is painted on the side of the storage bins. Unfortunately the markings on the bow plate that might have provided some clue as to the unit to which it was assigned are partially obscured by the leg of one of the crewmen.

A poorly retouched photo of an Sd.Kfz.251/7 Ausf.D framed in the wreckage of a burned out truck, clatters across a snowy field during the winter of 1944-45. These vehicles were assigned to the 3.Kompanie in each Pioniere battalion. The light assault bridges carried on each side were useful for crossing ditches or narrow streams during attacks.

The Sd.Kfz.251/17 Ausf.D armed with a 2cm KwK38 autocannon, is rarely seen in photographs. The gun was mounted on a pedestal and a small armored, open top turret that protected the operator surrounded the upper part.

A late production Marder III Ausf.M (Sd.Kfz.138) in Latvia during the summer of 1944. The early production vehicles featured a cast hood over the driver's position while later ones were made up of flat plates welded together like this one. The Marder III Ausf.M mounted the 7.5cm Pak40/3 on the modified chassis of the obsolete Pz.Kpfw.38(t) and was crewed by 4 men.

battery of Wespe self-propelled howitzers fires on enemy positions in the Soviet Union in August 1944. The Wespe carried the 10.5cm leFH18M gun mounted on a modified Pz.Kpfw.II chassis and had a crew of 5 men. They were issued to the Panzer-Artillerie-Regiments of the Panzer and Panzer-Grenadier-Divisions and first saw action at Kursk in July 1943.

Two Jagdpanzer 38(t) tank destroyers, sometimes referred to as the Hetzer, move into Warsaw during the Polish uprising in August 1944. Production of these vehicles started in April 1944 and the first combat units began to receive them by July 1944. Some were captured by the Polish combatants and used against the Germans during the battles in the city.

Late war Jagdpanzer 38(t) manufactured at the Skoda plant received an almost identical camouflage paint scheme of hard-edged wavy lines of Rotbraun RAL 8017 and Olivgrün RAL 6003 patches over the Dunkelgelb RAL 7028 base. Although it is not evident here due to the amount of dirt and mud on the wheels individual wheels were often completely painted in either of the two camouflage colors. This vehicle is an early version with the smaller, horizontal muffler.

A Jagdpanzer 38(t) and an Sd.Kfz.251/1Ausf.D advance across a muddy field in the spring of 1945. Due to the angle of the sun on the hull, it appears that the vehicle is painted in Dunkelgelb RAL 7028 but it is in fact painted in a camouflage scheme. Note the full squad of infantry seated in the half-track.

Two late model Jagdpanzer 38(t)s carry infantry across a muddy field in early 1945. The nearest vehicle is fitted with the later Flammenvernichter flame dampening exhaust system. In the background, a late Panther Ausf.G can be seen with its own version of the Flammenvernichter exhaust.

Two photos of the same Jagdpanzer 38(t), likely taken at the same time but in the second one, some Hungarian soldiers can be seen inspecting the abandoned vehicle. This Jagdpanzer is painted in a slightly different camouflage pattern than the previous photo but was also very common. A total of 2,584 of these vehicles were built from April 1944 to May 1945.

This StuG.III Ausf.G is fitted with the wide 'Winterkette' tracks that were introduced in the winter of 1942-43 to provide increased traction in deep snow. They were issued to units equipped with the StuG.III, Panzer III and some Panzer IV in the fall and were to be returned in the spring. This StuG.III Ausf.G has the waffle pattern Zimmerit coating that was applied only by the Alkett plant in Berlin.

These StuG.III Ausf.G have been fitted with the other wide track style, the 'Ostkette', which was first used in Russia in early 1944 to provide better flotation on soft ground and better traction in deep snow and were a bit narrower than the 'Winterkette' tracks. The lead StuG.III is a command vehicle and is fitted with the 2m Sternantenne behind the loader and also has the waffle pattern Zimmerit coating applied to it.

The crew of this StuG.III Ausf.G has added improvised spaced armor to the glacis of their vehicle using two armored covers from the engine deck of another StuG.III that had probably been knocked out. The cast 'topfblende' mantlet was introduced in November 1943 but never totally replaced the welded mantlet, which continued to be used up to the end of the war. The name 'Sperber' has been painted on the side of the mantlet, the meaning of which is unknown. Concrete reinforcement has been added to the sloping roof over the driver and on the right side. This photo was taken in September 1944.

oncrete reinforcement has been added to the sloping roof the superstructure on this StuG.III Ausf.G seen in Latvia in eptember 1944. Also visible in this photo is the shot eflector welded in front of the cupola that was introduced in ctober 1943. The opening in the MG shield was changed to rectangular shape to accommodate the larger sleeve on e MG 42 but this vehicle is still equipped with the MG 34.

A StuG.III Ausf.G passes an infantry squad huddled in a ditch in Rumania in late October 1944. The Schürzen have been field modified to hang on short pieces of pipe welded to the fenders. The plates were held in place with a cotter pin that allowed them to rotate freely when traveling through dense brush and which prevented them from being torn off and lost. A single or sometimes double plate was fixed on the side of the fighting compartment to protect the upper sides.

his late production StuG.III Ausf.G was manufactured after September 1944 when the application of Zimmerit was discontinued. It is also fitted with the ding gun travel lock on the glacis and single 80mm thick plate on the right side of the superstructure, which were introduced in July 1944. The remote MG ount, or Rundumfeuer, was introduced in April 1944 but shortages of the weapon meant that there were many vehicles issued without them. The loader's tches were redesigned to open to the sides to accommodate the device, which could be operated with safety from inside the vehicle using a periscopic ght.

This late StuG.III Ausf.G is fitted with the welded mantlet that has a hole in the upper left side to accommodate a coaxial MG that was introduced in July 194◄ Only one piece of Schürzen is left on the right side, illustrating the practicality of the modified hanger system seen in one of the previous photographs. Th▮ photograph was taken in Silesia in late March 1945.

A column of StuG.▮ Ausf.G, possibly fro▮ 3.SS-Panzer-Division 'Totenkopf', in Hunga▮ in January 194◄ Unusually, the vehicl◄ are carrying 'Oskett▮ spare tracks but are s▮ fitted with the standa▮ tracks with the i◄ chevrons. Both ha◄ new coats of wint◄ whitewash camouflag◄ paint applied in patche▮ leaving some of th▮ original paint showi▮ through. The gun trav◄ lock and waffle patte▮ Zimmerit place the ti▮ of manufacture sometime between Ju▮ and September 1944.

Three photos of a column of StuG.III Ausf.G somewhere on the Eastern Front in the late summer of 1944. The concrete reinforcement has been applied with an artistic flair and projects out around the driver's visor. Salvaged T-34 tracks have been hung on the spare track bracket on the front of one of the vehicles, probably because the wider track provides better protection. Usually, the Schürzen plates lapped front over back to prevent them from being snagged driving through dense brush but here they have been installed backwards.

This column of July-September 1944 production StuG.III Ausf.G have had a unique set of spaced armor plates added to the sides of the superstructure in place of the standard Schürzen .The gunner's seat can be seen laying on the forward edge of the roof. They are otherwise unremarkable except for the standard Bosch headlight fitted to the Notek light base on the glacis.

A StuG.IV from 277.StuG.Bde., photographed in East Prussia in February 1945 while Soviet troops mill around in the background. The StuG.IV was ordered into production in December 1943 to replace lost StuG.III production after the Alkett plant in Berlin was bombed. A total of 1,139 were produced from December 1943 to March 1945.

A StuG.III Ausf.G and a StuG.IV lay in a low flooded area, probably in the spring of 1945. An internal explosion has lifted the roof off the StuG.IV and deposited it upside down back on top of the vehicle. The StuG.III is one of those vehicles that received the modified Schürzen arrangement seen in previous photos.

A damaged StuG.IV waits for recovery or repair somewhere on the Eastern Front in the winter of 1944-45. The left drive sprocket can be seen laying on the glacis. The absence of Zimmerit places the date of manufacture sometime after September 1944.

This new StuG.III Ausf.G was manufactured after Zimmerit had been discontinued September 1944 but appears not to have the travel lock that was introduced in July of that year. Note the hand warmers on the motorcycle combination traveling beside the StuG.III.

A column of Pz.Kpfw.IV Ausf.H or Ausf.J on the outskirts of an East Prussian town in the summer of 1944. They are probably new issue as there does n[...] appear to be any battle damage and they carry a full set of Schürzen. The single Bosch headlight on the left fender is an identifying feature of the Panzer I[...] Ausf.H or J, as there were two headlights on the Panzer IV Ausf.G.

A Pz.Kpfw.IV Ausf.J with an Sd.Kfz.251/3 Ausf.C on the Eastern Front during the summer of 1944. The tactical numbers on the turret Schürzen are probabl[...] red with a white outline compared to the black center of the national cross. The Sd.Kfz.251/3 mittlere Funkpanzerwagen has a 2m Sternantenne attached [...] a mount on the rear plate and was used for the FuG8 radio set.

A Pz.Kpfw.IV Ausf.H or Ausf.J from I./Pz.Rgt.23 of 23.Panzer-Division in Nyíregyháza, Hungary in October 1944 after being transferred from Poland. The division fought in Hungary throughout the rest of the war, gradually falling back through Slovenia to the Graz area of Austria before being overrun by Soviet forces.

A group of SS-Panzer-Grenadiers hitch a ride on a battle weary Pz.Kpfw.IV Ausf.J somewhere on the Eastern Front during the winter of 1944-45. All of the soldiers are wearing the SS fur lined anorak first issued the previous winter. The Panzer IV has a hastily applied coat of white winter camouflage paint.

A 15cm Schwere Panzerhaubitz auf Geschutzwagen III/IV (Sf) (Sd.Kfz.165) 'Hummel' self propelled howitzer from I./Pz.Art.Rgt.73 of 1.Panzer-Division in Tarnopol during the spring of 1944. The Hummel carried the 15cm sFH18/ heavy howitzer mounted on a lengthened Panzer IV chassis. They were issued to the heavy batteries of the Panzer-Artillerie-Regiments and first saw action at Kursk in 1943. The light framework in front of the driver's position was used to aid the driver in lining up the vehicle for firing.

This early Hummel has been fitted with the wide 'Winterkette' tracks used exclusively on the Eastern Front. In early 1944, the extended housing for the driver was extended across the full width of the hull to provide additional space for the radio operator. There were six guns in a battery and it was common to see the position of each gun identified by a painted letter, in this case, an 'A', indicating that this was the first gun in the battery.

A late production Sturmpanzer IV (Sd.Kfz.166) 'Brummbär' from Stu.Pz.Kp.z.b.V.218 photographed in Warsaw, Poland during the summer of 1944. This unit was formed in early August 1944 and transferred to Army Group Center with 10 Sturmpanzer IV to assist against the uprising. The unit was destroyed in January 1945 before it could be fully organized as Stu.Pz.Abt.218.

A pair of late production Sturmpanzer IV 'Brummbär' knocked out somewhere on the Eastern Front in the spring of 1945. These vehicles were manufactured sometime after September 1944 when the application of Zimmerit was discontinued. Of particular interest is the unusual return roller mounts on the nearest 'Brummbär'. Instead of the standard cast mount, they have been manufactured out of welded plates. This type of mount has been observed on other late Panzer IVs, including a Panzer IV preserved at a Czech museum, and is believed to have been a stopgap solution necessitated by a shortage of cast mounts.

A group of weary Hungarian soldiers are marched into captivity by Soviet troops past a Panzer IV/70(V) (Sd.Kfz.162/1), often referred to as a Jagdpanzer IV 'Lang', in early 1945. The first Panzer IV/70(V) were issued in August 1944 making this one of the early production vehicles manufactured before the discontinuation of Zimmerit in September 1944.

These Panther Ausf.A from I./Panzer-Regiment 'Großdeutschland' are being loaded for transport to East Prussia in early August 1944 to meet the threat the Russian summer offensive, Operation 'Bagration'. The division was equipped with 79 Panthers in July 1944.

66

Two Panther Ausf.A from I./Panzer-Regiment 'Großdeutschland' raise clouds of dust crossing a field in East Prussia during the summer of 1944. The tactical number, '413', can be seen on the rear quarter of the turret, probably painted in black with a thin white outline.

A Panther Ausf.G from I./SS-Pz.Rgt.1 of 1.SS-Panzer-Division 'LSSAH' photographed in the Gran bridgehead area of Hungary during Operation Südwind in late February or early March 1945. The Panther is fitted with the vertical 'Flammenvernichter' flame dampening exhaust and raised cooling fan tower used to provide heat to the crew compartment in cold weather.

A Panther Ausf.A from I./SS-Pz.Rgt.3 of 3.SS-Panzer-Division 'Totenkopf', in the Kovel area of Poland during the summer of 1944. Other photos of this Panther show it had the tactical number '111' painted in white on the turret. The division's skull emblem can be faintly seen painted in white to the left of the MG mount. Another commonly seen divisional marking, a white triangle, can be seen on the rear turret access hatch on the Panther in the background.

This early Panther Ausf.A from I.SS-Pz.Rgt.5 of 5.SS-Panzer-Division 'Wiking' was photographed the summer of 1944. The divisional emblem a rounded swastika has been painted white in a white outline black shield on a bare patch of the glacis plate. Note how small arms fire and shell splinters have chipped off the Zimmerit coating leaving areas of bare steel and red primer.

Panther Ausf.G from I./Pz.Rgt.31 from 5.Panzer-Division near the East Prussian city of Goldap in the autumn of 1944. It is painted in the factory applied 'ambush' scheme that was authorized in August and September 1944. The numbers on the turret are red with a white outline but the reflection caused by the angle of the sun makes them appear white.

Another Panther Ausf.G from I./Pz.Rgt.31 of 5.Panzer-Division. In this photo, the white outlined red numbers on the turret are more apparent. Also of note is the red outline painted around the national cross on the rear stowage bin. This is a peculiarity seen in many Panzer IVs and Panthers of this division.

No fewer than eighteen German soldiers can be counted riding on this Zimmerit coated Panther Ausf.G from Panzer-Brigade 109 photographed in Hungary in the fall of 1944. Ten new Panzer-Brigades were formed in early July 1944, each organized with 33 Panthers in a Panzer-Abteilung, 11 Pz.IV/70(V) in a Panzer-Jäger-Kompanie and 3 Panthers and four Flakpanzer in the Panzer-Abteilung Stab. Panzer-Brigade 109 was to have a short history however, as it was disbanded and integrated into Pz.Gren.Div.FHH in October 1944.

A Panther Ausf.G from an unknown Army unit, photographed after arriving at the Baltic port of Memel, Lithuania in early December 1944. Telltale signs previous battles can be seen in the form of shrapnel holes in the gun cleaning rod storage tube mounted on the side of the tank. Russian forces surrounde the port in October 1944 and strong German resistance prevented them from taking the city until 27 January 1945.

This damaged early Panther Ausf.D was captured in a Czechoslovakian rail yard in May 1945. The commander's cupola, along with the complete gu assembly, is missing. The first outer road wheel has been reinforced with additional rivets between the rim bolts whereas the last three stations still have th original sixteen-bolt configuration.

Troops from 21.Feld-Division (Luftwaffe) take cover behind a Tiger I from s.Pz.Abt.510 near Akmene, Lithuania in the summer of 1944. The battalion insignia, a rampant bear on a shield can be seen on the rear plate just behind the helmet of the man on the right. This unit painted the tactical numbers on the left and right rear quarters of the turret in black numbers with a white outline.

The crew of this mid-production Tiger I from an unknown unit, work to cover their vehicle with cut foliage to help camouflage it from air attack. The rubber tired road wheels and the shape of the front point identify this vehicle as being manufactured before spring 1944.

Tiger crewmen enjoy an impromptu outdoor piano concert in the fall of 1944. Unfortunately, no markings are visible that would identify the Tiger battalion to which they belong.

This Tiger II from 3./s.Pz.Abt.501, is pictured here abandoned after th fighting in the Weichsel bend on 2 October 1944. At the beginning of Octobe the unit received some Tigers transferred from s/Pz.Abt.509, which brough their complement up to 36 combat ready tanks.

A Tiger I being towe out of roadside ditch b another Tiger. This wa officially frowned upor as the danger existe that the strain could als incapacitate the towin vehicle leaving tw vehicles unserviceable The Tiger in th foreground has th tactical marking for th battalion commander, black 'I' with a whit outline, painted on th side of the turre Judging by the absenc of a visible tactica number on the side the turret of the othe Tiger, they are likel from s.Pz.Abt.510 which carried thei markings on the rea quarters of the turret.

After the war, the Soviets recovered this ex-s.SS-Pz.Abt.502 Tiger II from Kummersdorf and used it as a range target, a fate that befell many of the surviving Panzer on all fronts.